A PSYCHOLOGICAL SURVIVAL GUIDE FOR BREAST CANCER

Dr Phil Watts

Copyright © 2015

The moral right of Dr Phil Watts to be indentified as the Author and Laila Savolainen as the Cover Artist of the work has been asserted by them in accordance with the Copyright, Designs and Patents Act 1988 (UK). All rights reserved. No part of this book may be used or reproduced, stored in a retrieval system, or transmitted in any form, or by any means electronic, mechanical, recording, photocopying, or in any manner whatsoever without permission in writing from the publisher, except for the inclusions of brief quotations in a review.

National Library of Australia Cataloguing-in-Publication entry

Creator:	Watts, Phil, 1962- author.
Title:	A psychological survival guide for breast cancer / PhilipWatts; edited by Linda McNamara.
ISBN:	9780992412111 (paperback)
ISBN:	9780992412128 (ebook)
Subjects:	Breast-Cancer-Psychological aspects.
	Breast-Cancer-Patients-Care-Australia.

Other Creators/Contributors:
Editing: Linda McNamara

Book Cover Design: Pickawoowoo, Laila Savolainen
Interior Design: Pickawoowoo Publishing Group
Dewey Number: 616.994490994

Printed & Channel Distribution
Lightning Source | Ingram (USA/UK/EUROPE/AUS)

DEDICATION

I dedicate this book to one of my greatest heroes, and best friend, my wife Bethwyn.

TABLE OF CONTENTS

Dedication iii
Acknowledgements vii
Preface..ix
Introduction xi
Shattered... 1
Everybody's Different 5
Emotional Rollercoaster 7
Aftershock 11
YPB Look 17
Toughen Up 21
Alternative Therapy and "Conspiracy" 23
What is Cancer? 29
Medical Specialists 35
Decisions in a Crisis 39
Information Overload 43
Positive Attitude.. 47
Talking to People 51
Trauma.. 57
Surviving Treatment 61
Chemotherapy Horrors 67
Losing Hair and Other Losses 73
Breasts 79
Make Your Peace 85
The Practical... 89

It's Back!	91
Forgetting To Live	95
Partner's Reactions – Shared Experience	99
Children	105
Humour and Writing	111
Funerals	115
Conclusion	117

ACKNOWLEDGEMENTS

Unlike every other book I have written, I wanted not only to share what I have learnt, but to help others who have to walk where I have walked. Life is a teacher, and my experiences have shown me the terrible need for the information in this book. In my more optimistic moments I acknowledge how life's trials make us stronger, but I also acknowledge how cruel some of those trials seem. I am glad that I have been able to convert my experience into something which may help others.

One great mind who willingly read the book to make sure it was medically correct was Dr Daphne Tsoi, a medical oncologist at St John of God Hospital in Murdoch and Subiaco Western Australia. I appreciate Dr Tsoi sharing some ideas which could be incorporated into this book. While she is not someone who reads self-help books she could recognise the value of this material to others.

There are many great hands which help put books together. Julie-Ann Harper, managing director of Pick-a-woowoo Publishing Group, and Linda McNamara, my editor and proof reader extraordinaire, were instrumental in turning words into text. I cannot thank them enough for their help with my projects.

Books are hard to write without the help and tolerance of those who are closest to you. I appreciate all that my family does to enable me to achieve my goals. My children are loving and supportive of me doing good works. My wife is patient, loving and encouraging. As you will discover as you read the book, her experiences have been central to my learning. She is a most remarkable example of how someone can show dignity, grace and style in otherwise horrendous circumstances.

PREFACE

Brave is not a word I like to hear in relation to people suffering from cancer. It is a cliché used without thought. You don't choose to get cancer, and having the treatment does not make you brave. There is no choice – you have to do it. "Brave" does not allow you to feel – nor does it allow others to realise what is going on.

Of course there is bravery at times, but I think that you also demonstrate a lot of other things: feelings such as being frightened, angry, sad, lonely and depressed; and characteristics such as being dignified, resourceful and having a fighting spirit. Sometimes you feel all of these things in a day, while some may never apply to you. In other words, you are a unique woman having an individual, albeit multifaceted, experience.

This book is designed for one purpose: to give you permission to experience the journey in the way in which you need to do it. You need to be able to experience this cancer and its treatment with all the resources you can muster. I want to help you to see that to undertake the journey your way, there are

Preface

some things about psychology that can help you.

Psychological information can help you to understand why you feel the way you do, and provide practical advice on how to deal with certain situations. It helps to understand something about grief and trauma, doctors and medicine, emotions and psychology.

I hope that this gives you a quick overview of those things you will need to deal with. I did not want to write a long or detailed book, as you already have too much to worry about. My goal was to keep this short and to the point, practical and succinct.

Some of the things in the book are grim, but anyone who has cancer will have grim thoughts (when they stop long enough to think). It is preferable that someone says something about those things.

INTRODUCTION

If you are reading this, I am so sorry. You have embarked on a journey that is rocking your world. Whether you are the person diagnosed with cancer, a partner, a family member, or a caring friend, I wish that you did not need a book like this. However, in a world surrounded by experts, someone has to help you understand why you feel the way you do, and what might underlie the choices you need to make.

The closer you are to the cancer (the person diagnosed, spouse or family), the greater the likelihood that you are spiralling out of control at an emotional level while trying to deal with all of the urgent medical issues. Symbolically, you are you a bit like a duck on a lake – trying to appear serene to all those with whom you deal, while under the water your emotional feet are paddling like crazy.

I have written this book as if I am talking to the person who has been diagnosed with cancer, however, I have also written it to help all of those people who help the person who has been diagnosed. Therefore, please understand that while this book

Introduction

can be helpful to all people in a supporting role, I have it written for the central player who has the most important role in this situation: the person diagnosed with cancer.

Why do you need this book? Medical specialists have a hard enough job managing their speciality – they do not necessarily have time for emotions. Everyone else is dealing with their own reactions. Where do you get help? How do you know what to do? What should you do to get by?

I have written this book to help you to get a little bit of sanity and direction back into your life. It is not a complete work, but a collection of practical ideas to help you cope, keep going, and perhaps even remain psychologically sane. Therefore, this is a psychological survival guide.

My first and most essential key point is that this is your journey and no one can tell you how to undertake it. I want to give you permission to do it your way (which is often the opposite of how we live our lives – giving to others). The problem is that for everyone life is short. With you staring down the barrel of uncertainty, the need to live a full life with no regrets is essential.

As much as you may like to, you cannot rewind these moments of time. You have to go forward and not look back, especially if looking back comes with "if only" regrets. Therefore this book is short. I want you to read it in a day or two so that you are not wasting precious time going down the wrong path.

I have written this book from two perspectives. The first is as a psychologist who has worked with people dealing with different emotional conditions. As a psychologist I am a student of human behaviour, interested in processes and pathways. More significantly, however, I wrote this book from the perspective of a husband who has twice watched his wife's diagnosis and treatment for breast cancer, while trying to help her survive as a person and all of us to cope as a family. I have also watched the impact from my mother-in-law passing away from the same cancer, and how the damage from that experience reverberated through the family both at the time and some two decades later. The damage of her passing has caused a lasting legacy of dysfunction, some of which may have been able to be avoided with some common-sense advice early in the process.

The purpose of this book, however, is not for me to share my war stories, but to provide you with practical help and examples - to help you make sense of, and deal with, the events which will transpire from this moment onwards. I am not the navigator, I am merely the explorer who has walked this path

Introduction

and noticed some of the scenery. You need to blaze your own trail. However, there are some parts of the journey which are the same for most people and there are psychological aspects which are known and predictable.

My writing style is direct, full of examples, and loaded with practical suggestions. I apologise if any of it offends or triggers emotions. I am not trying to hurt but to heal. However if I do not say something about some of the hard topics, who else will?

I do not know at which point you got this book. I hope it is at an early stage in your journey because it will give you a chance to put a few structures in place while you are busy doing all of the things that the medical profession requires.

SHATTERED

The exact moment of knowing varies from person to person. For some, it is sitting in the specialist's office as he or she opens the file on the desk and utters the words *"it's cancer"*. Your specialist may tell you in a factual way, perhaps pausing for a few moments in compassion, before getting into an explanation of your options. Chances are that you will miss most of what was said after those first words as your brain reacts with a sudden surge of adrenaline – fight, flight or freeze! None of those reactions allow you to really take in what the good doctor is telling you.

For many of you, the realisation occurred at an earlier stage. Perhaps you found a lump and, with a sinking feeling or a sense of foreboding, realised that something was wrong. Perhaps you went for a scan and the chatty, friendly radiologist suddenly went quiet or called in a doctor or other specialist for a second opinion. Maybe there was an incidental finding when you had a regular scan, or a scan for some other condition.

However it happened, the dark news is staring

you in the face – cancer. In psychological research when someone wants to trigger the brain into negative emotions they flash certain words on a screen. Those words cause the brain to react faster than it would if nice words like love, happy or joy were used. The negative words used in brain reaction studies are words like blood, death, hate and, of course, cancer. Cancer is a word which comes with many strong connotations which are deeply embedded in the human psyche – something that occurs long before your cancer diagnosis.

Psychological research on memory talks about a category of events which are vividly remembered at the moment they happen. These are called 'flashbulb memories'. People recall when the planes hit the Twin Towers, John Lennon was assassinated, or the Space Shuttle Challenger disintegrated on take-off. People recollect the events with vivid detail of what they were doing, wearing, thinking or feeling at the moment they heard the news.

In the same way, a flashbulb explodes in your mind as the cancer diagnosis and realisation takes place. At this moment, your life has been changed forever. This change may be anything from a short term derailment, through to your life turning into a catastrophic train wreck.

The first people on the scene are the medical

specialists, because you are in need of urgent medical intervention and time is of the essence. However, you are also in need of some guidance and direction to make sense of what is happening to you – some psychological first aid. Simple answers to questions such as who do you tell, or guidance in relation to how you react to others is required. The following chapters will provide you with some of that psychological first aid.

As your treatments start, the weeks roll forward. The serious business of surviving becomes central to you. Medical treatment is never easy and the more serious your cancer, the more brutal the treatment. Questions run through your mind such as: *"What is happening? How should I cope? Are my feelings normal?"* This book will help you to survive this second phase.

Hopefully your treatment eventually stops. You will then be on observation regimes. Now is the time to take stock of the longer term situation. Survival mode got you through, but life keeps going. Questions which were not able to be asked during the initial crisis now need to be looked at. These questions include: *"What is the meaning of my life? How have I been permanently changed? What else should I do?"* These are all important things to consider.

Action Summary:-

- Your brain has recorded events in a flash-bulb-like manner. Make sure that you write them out in a journal or diary so you do not have to keep rehearsing them in your head. Writing is often a good way to let go.

- Survival mode helps you to survive, but at some point you have to shift from survival mode to living again. They are two distinct psychological states, but knowing that they exist is what matters now. Understanding the difference can come later.

- Feeling overwhelmed and shocked by the news? Tell yourself you are completely normal to feel that way.

EVERYBODY'S DIFFERENT

If you were to ask me to say exactly what you are feeling right now, as a psychologist with 25 years' experience, I would tell you that I do not know. However, plenty of well-meaning friends, family and strangers are going to tell you what you are feeling, and how you should act.

The reason I cannot tell you exactly what you are feeling right now is because everybody is different. While there are some common patterns of emotions people will experience in these situations, everybody will experience them in different ways and at different times, and not everybody will experience all of the same processes in the same way. If you have lost a family member to cancer, then your experience is markedly different to someone whose family member survived. Your internal map is completely different. We all know that cancer can kill people so everyone has some element of fear, however, if you have watched someone you love die of the condition, it can make your internal map so much more disturbing.

My first rule for surviving this experience is that you must do it *"your way"*. Don't let anybody else tell you how you should go through this experience.

You have to make the best choices you can, and act according to those choices, knowing that it is you who has to live with the day-to-day situation.

For women who have devoted their lives to others (such as the husband and kids), this can be a hard line to understand:- You need to think about what you need, rather than what everyone else needs. However, you must be the one who has no regrets about the time you have. I am not advocating that you be selfish and disregard the others you are close to, but that you be firm about what you need.

Action Summary:-

- Everyone around you thinks that they are an expert on what is best for you! Pick your advice carefully or you will be overwhelmed.

- Rule number 1 – Do it your way! Nothing is more important in this process than you realising that it is your life and your experience – you have to make the choices in relation to how you deal with the experience.

- Be firm to ensure that you get what you need. I am not saying that you should become selfish, but you must put your priority on your own emotional and physical needs in a way that you might never have done before.

EMOTIONAL ROLLERCOASTER

The human brain, a fantastic device which has evolved over millennia, helps us to survive. Effectively, there are three broad pathways to the way in which the brain functions. The first is called the brain stem. This is the basic primitive brain which controls heart rate, breathing and other reflex-like responses. Over the top of the brain stem are areas which are linked together in a complex system called the limbic system. The limbic system is associated with emotional processing. One part of the limbic system is the amygdala. This walnut-sized part of the brain is the fear centre and is used to alert the body to dangers and arousal. Over the top of the brain is the wrinkly grey matter. This is called the cortex. The cortex is associated with thinking and reasoning.

The moment you heard the word cancer, the amygdala part of your brain activated intense emotional responses. As the limbic system fired up, your thinking and reasoning diminished. There is every chance that you have not remembered most of what the doctor told you because your body was on arousal overload. Therefore, while you may be able to tell me the colour of the doctor's office and the smell of the doctor's after-shave or perfume, you probably won't be able to accurately recall much of what the doctor told you.

Several very important pieces of information arise from this initial understanding of the brain. First, do not go alone to see your doctor. Second, make sure you take good notes. The person you take with you to see the doctor will be an auxiliary cortex (that is, if you do not get my psycho-speak, they are your spare brain) – they can remember and hear things for you (although they will probably have their own fear reactions). Jotting down key points will help you to remember facts, figures and percentages which are going to be incredibly relevant to you.

What is happening here could loosely be called "shock". Thinking is low and emotional arousal is high. In nature, when there is a threat, all creatures exhibit one of three classes of behaviour. These are fight, flight or freeze. Fight means to want to try and fight it and beat it; flight means to try to run away; and freeze means to become paralysed by fear. Which behaviour did you experience?

Because the brain is in limbic system overload, thinking is not happening. In fact, the brain actively works to shut down thinking. There are various techniques the brain uses and some of the most common ones are denial (*"this can't be real"*, *"it's not happening"*, *"the doctor's got it wrong"*, *"there must be a mistake"*). All of these types of thoughts are completely common and normal, and they serve to delay the onset of the next stages of grief.

It is important that you recognise that you can experience any one of these different stages because it will take a while for your brain to accept what is going on. Unfortunately, some people never move past these stages and have a whole array of patterns of behaviour which can be quite dysfunctional.

Action Summary:-

- Bad news triggers a strong emotional reaction. As emotion increases, thinking decreases. Therefore, to ensure that you remember critical information, bring a friend or write notes when you see your specialists.

- Are you aware of which shock reaction you are having? Are you in fright – overwhelmed by fear and unable to deal with issues; freeze – paralysed by fear and unable to even function; or fight – angry at someone or something following the diagnosis? Now that you are aware of what you are doing, who is on the receiving end and is your reaction appropriate? For example, are you directing your anger at the nurse?

- To work out the appropriateness of your reactions, the simple gauge is trigger and response. If the trigger is small and your response is small then that is normal. If the trigger is big (such are rescheduling the operation on the day you attend hospital) and your response is big, then that is probably appropriate. However, if you are biting the receptionist's head off because they can only fit you in at 4pm instead of 2pm next month, you are directing your anger at her unfairly.

AFTERSHOCK

The journey that follows is one which is going to raise a myriad of emotions. Sometimes this kaleidoscope of feelings takes place within seconds or minutes. Sometimes it will cycle over days, months and even years.

As the shock wears off and reality sets in, some of the emotions you are likely to experience include bargaining, sadness, anger and fear. Let us look at these feelings.

Bargaining is a common early stage reaction. People want to bargain with God or the universe (*"I'll be more religious, more worthy, kinder, if you'll let me live"*). If the bargaining doesn't work, then people may become angry at God or the universe. Either way, the early stage of bargaining is quite a marked feature for those experiencing cancer.

The psychological purpose of bargaining is control. If you can do something, anything to make a difference, then you feel more in control. It is good to look at what you can do, but making a bargain with the universe or God does not cure cancer. Being close to God can bring comfort to religious people, and making bargains can allow you to feel some control.

Sadness and grief are a critical component of dealing with any type of loss. Depending upon what transpires with your cancer, there are a number of losses. There are real losses (including the loss of hair, loss of time, the financial cost, or loss of a sex life) and potential losses (such as the fear of dying). There are also a lot of subtle losses associated with the loss of the life you used to have – the loss of certainty of the future and so on. I will talk more about some of these losses later.

For quality of life, it helps to be able to resolve some of these losses. Even just acknowledging that they exist, and being able to cry about the loss, can help to relieve some of the pressure.

Asking "*why me?*" is an essential stage of grief and trauma. It is often experienced in the early stages, however, it can occur at any stage. The purpose of self-blame is control. If you can work out why, maybe you can change something and therefore make a difference. The harsh reality is that there is no reason why. This is you and that is all there is to it. You've had bad luck, and in some cases bad genes, but effectively there is no reason why you have cancer.

Anger is also another aspect of this process. This could be anger at what has happened, feeling that this is unfair, and anger from being sick and in pain. In the chemo ward or radiation centre you will sometimes see people responding in anger. Unfortunately, this anger is often misplaced and staff and others are being abused because the anger is coming from someone's fear and hurt.

I like to conceptualise anger as a secondary emotion. It exists to cover underlying feelings, typically sadness. When the sadness is addressed, the anger often dissipates.

If anger and sadness are predominant features, then undergoing some psychological counselling can assist with quality of life, and antidepressant medications can help a number of people deal with negative feelings of both anger and depression. However, during the treatment phase people are often too busy to deal with these things.

One of the hardest aspects of dealing with cancer is that getting through the medical treatment is the first priority. This often delays the grief process. Sometimes grief is delayed for days, weeks, months or even years, because people have to get through their next dose of chemotherapy or radiation or surgery. Recognising that you are delaying grief can be helpful.

Fear is perhaps one of the worst aspects of this experience. Prior to getting cancer, if you got an ache in the back or a small lump somewhere, you would have immediately thought that it was just an ache or a lump. After being diagnosed with cancer, people automatically see the worst and panic in case it is a secondary cancer or a new cancer somewhere else. Most people I have come across do not ever return to their pre-cancer state of relaxation. They have a sense of hypervigilance.

As outlined, there is a kaleidoscope of emotions. I have only mentioned some of the broad-brush families of emotion. Within each of these are many subtle shades and variations. The bottom line for you is that cancer has triggered a lot of emotion and reduced logic and thinking.

Action Summary:-

- ◆ The stages of grief are different for everyone but most people visit some or all of the stages at some point. These stages include denial, bargaining, anger, sadness and depression. You need to constantly check which of these emotions you are experiencing because it will affect how you deal with things. Each stage needs to be acknowledged.

- Bargaining – you need to realise that by trying to be better, kinder, more religious or whatever else you promise, you are trying to regain control of an uncontrollable situation. By all means be better, but do not expect it to provide a cure.

- *"Why me?"* is a similar variation of the need to regain control. If there is something wrong with you, and you can change it, you feel more in control. The reality is that there may be no *"why me"* – it is just bad luck and bad genes. Even if it was something to do with you, it is too late now so aim to move forward not back.

- Grief and sadness are real. A large trauma study which examined different coping mechanisms concluded that the age-old advice to have a cry really does help! Allow yourself time to cry. It is okay to be sad.

- Anger is a destructive emotion. It is important to recognise that it is a stage of grief and needs to worked be through. Anger is related to the "fight" part of the brain's functioning, but you need to fight the cancer not your helpers. If you are stuck feeling angry or sad, then consider getting some counselling.

YPB LOOK

You bump into an old friend at a supermarket who you have not seen for some time. They ask how you are going and, in the course of responding, you stumble out the word "cancer" – and then you see it – the YPB look ("*You Poor Bitch*").

Telling people that you have cancer is one of the hardest situations that you will ever face. There are several reasons why this is so difficult. The YPB look is the first aspect. People who love and care for you are genuinely going to be shocked and distressed to find out the news. Here you are in a time of your life when you are most vulnerable, your emotions are running high, you are struggling to cope, and now your friend or acquaintance is distressed and emotionally aroused over what you have just told them.

People you tell can have one of two common reactions. The first is their own emotional reaction. This is because they love and care for you, they have been through cancer, what you told them threatens their mortality, or they have some other underlying reason. Therefore, you are the one who has just been diagnosed and now you have to soothe and comfort another person around their emotions.

A second type of reaction is that they are genuinely concerned about you and therefore may start asking questions about how you are going and how you are coping. The chances are you were coping by being able to suppress and put terrible thoughts into a box deep within your mind. Their well-meaning comments have now tumbled your emotion to the surface. The more genuinely concerned they are about you, the easier it is for you to feel like crying.

The options you have to deal with others are limited, in the sense that you cannot identify and talk to everybody who needs to know. However, it is important that you find ways of talking to the people who care about you. Everybody's different, but one of the ways people find effective is to nominate a friend as a spokesperson who contacts others on your behalf. Most people will understand if your spokesperson gives a short explanation to the effect that you are finding it too emotional to talk about this situation yourself.

In this day and age, some people use technology to set up online areas, such as Facebook pages, outlining their treatment. The trouble with this is that the minute people see the comments, they will want to contact you to find out further details and offer support. Therefore, if you put out any sort of written brief, it is critical that it includes instructions detailing what you need.

Avoidance is a common response. My family go to church. My wife found it very hard to go to church because many of the 120 people she has known throughout her life wanted to ask how she was. I simply let her avoid going until she was ready to go. Prior to going to church I also gave a small announcement outlining a little about what she needed.

Coupled with avoidance, when people are traumatised they often need to speak about things (and need to keep speaking about it). You will also have the urge to talk about things emotionally. Therefore, it is important that you find people who are psychologically mature enough to be able to cope with you talking about your feelings. In simple terms, be selective in who you talk to about your feelings.

A strategy a number of people find helpful is to share pieces of the picture with different people – one person to talk to about your fears, another about concerns relating to medication, and somebody else about how the situation is impacting upon your relationships. That way, rather than one person being burdened with too much, the information is shared and the responsibility is diffused.

Action Summary:-

- Telling people you have cancer is one of the most difficult things you have to do because other people may have intense reactions which you then have to deal with. Find strategies to share the news which do not make you the first line contact. Have a trusted friend or contact provide information on your behalf. Use technology to update others on your status. We are all different, so find the way which works best for you.

- Avoidance is a common way of managing people. In the short term, some avoidance is a good strategy. Let yourself feel stronger before facing larger groups of friends or family. However, long-term avoidance escalates fears (face a fear and it gets better, avoid a fear and it gets worse).

- Share the load. Find a few psychologically mature people who understand you and tell them some or all of what you need to say. A couple of good friends to talk to are worth their weight in gold!

TOUGHEN UP

While the YPB reaction is emotionally overwhelming, at least it has arisen because people either care about you or about the emotions of the situation. Sadly, there are other people who are just plain inappropriate.

You can often spot these people pushing their way through the crowd to come to you when they see you. They want to tell you about a particular diet, ask inappropriate questions about your treatment, tell you not to use modern medicine, share horror stories of a relative who lived, died or was treated successfully using some strange means of treatment.

I am astonished at some people's lack of insight and tact, but it is a sad reality of what you need to deal with. Ultimately, my advice on this is that you need to "toughen up". In toughening up I am talking about being able to set boundaries and put limits on this sort of behaviour. Do not let people dump things onto you. You need to get better at being able to hold up your hand and say *"stop, I don't need to hear this"*, and then change the subject.

I would argue that when it comes to situations like cancer, everybody is an expert and it seems that everybody has had some distant relative survive through the use of miraculous treatments. If you think there is any benefit in what they are saying, tell them to email you the information so that you can choose to look at it in your own time, when you are ready to deal with it.

Action Summary:-

- Learn to be firm about unwanted advice. Tell people to put it in an email, or tell them you are not interested. Do whatever it takes to look after yourself.

- See the intent (to help you) so that you can treat others with respect, but you have to keep your boundaries to protect yourself. In extreme cases, you may need to tell others that you do not need to hear what they want to say, or even walk away from them.

ALTERNATIVE THERAPY AND "CONSPIRACY"

The sad reality of cancer is that it is a serious condition without a simple cure. There are various treatments which have been appropriately researched and found to improve survival rates. As discussed elsewhere, some of this treatment is quite brutal but has been shown to improve the ability to survive.

However, where there is uncertainty in how to fix a problem, there are often multiple alternative explanations. Generally speaking, the fewer explanations there are, the more effective the cure. When science does not know how to cure, multiple explanations arise.

This has given rise to all sorts of conspiracy theories and, while there are many variations, the conspiracy theories run along the lines of the big pharmaceutical companies not wanting cancer treatments to be produced because the companies will not make money. These theories sound very plausible and have a small element of truth (drugs are expensive to produce so the companies need to make a profit) but the point I would like to make is that part of the reason for the existence of these theories is that they are an elaborate form of psychological denial.

If there is a conspiracy to hide the real way to treat a condition, and the proponents of the conspiracy typically endorse particular types of alternative treatment, then there is some hope that the alternative treatment can work. You will get better and not die. I do not know anyone who has had cancer who does not want to live, and therefore most people would be willing to do almost anything for that to happen.

We know that with alternative medicine, some folk remedies have been found to be valid. For example, willow bark tea was once used to treat headaches. Eventually science identified the component, which is a now a common pharmaceutical (Aspirin). A cure for certain types of cancer may eventually be found through alternative medicines, but at this stage it is speculative rather than evidence-based. Once a cure is found, it will become the treatment of choice available to the public. It will probably get the doctor a Noble prize.

I also would argue that treatments such as chemotherapy take a horrendous toll on the body's various systems and I can see no reason why supplements, vitamins and so on would not assist in recovery and improving the quality of life. Therefore, there are in fact some health-based things which can help you. However, get good advice about what to take and how much of it is a good thing (some herbs can even be toxic in high doses).

Into the mix I would add another psychological factor: control. If you have control over something then it helps you to feel less anxious. You cannot control the chemotherapy or the cancer, but you can control diet and supplements. By hoping that they work, and being able to control some part of your life, it makes you feel more powerful in this powerless situation.

When we put all of these pieces together, there is 'quackery' and also things which may be of assistance, but be careful about investing emotional time and energy into unorthodox, unhealthy or excessive treatments in the hope that they will cure your cancer, especially on the basis of conspiracy evidence.

The most important decisions for you to make are quality of life decisions. If you end up having 6 months left to live, would eating only raw vegetables and having 3 day fasts be the best way to use this time when there is no evidence that either of these techniques are beneficial? If you want to try such techniques, you need to understand that you are

Alternative Therapy and "Conspiracy"

doing it out of hope, or a need to control something when you feel powerless, and it may involve a form of denial. If you still want to do these things, then it is your right to do so because this is your journey.

Action Summary:-

- Conspiracy theories abound. Alternative treatments are plentiful. They exist because there is no simple answer to cancer. You need to understand that if you embark on alternative treatment or invest in conspiracy theories you are engaging in something to help you cope but might not make any difference. In the case of some types of treatment, they might even make your situation worse. My advice is to choose carefully how you spend your time and money. Understand the psychology that feeling powerless and out of control feeds the need for something, anything, which might work. We will do anything for hope.

- The internet is wonderful device for research but unfortunately it has no capacity to tell you want is or is not true. Therefore, research treatment options, but be careful about how much weight you put on what you find. A wise consumer considers options based on evidence and fact. A foolish consumer makes decisions on emotions and hope.

- If you want to try alternative treatments, you need to understand that you are trying them based on hope – a need to control something when you feel powerless – and it may involve a form of denial. It is your journey. If you still want to try these things, make the best choice you can but with the knowledge that you cannot get this time back again.

WHAT IS CANCER?

My neighbour, who is a basic sort of bloke, described cancer as *"human rust"*. Another acquaintance, who is into natural medicine, said *"cancer is a word not a sentence"*. However you conceptualise cancer, there are some things you need to know in order to understand what you are going through.

Effectively cancer means that the cells grow rapidly. In a perfect model, these cells double at abnormal rates. Therefore, one cell becomes two, then four, eight, sixteen, thirty-two, sixty-four, and so on. The speed they grow relates to the aggressiveness of the cancer. For example, bowel cancers are often very slow-growing whereas some types of breast cancers can be very aggressive and double in size quite rapidly.

As the cells double in size they need food and nutrients to survive. Therefore they hijack blood supply from other cells. The ability of cells to access nutrition may affect the rate of doubling. What causes the cells to double at abnormal rates is one of the areas which is being explored in cancer research.

We know that in some cases genes assist in making cells abnormal, but that is not the only reason.

As cells get bigger they start to infuse the tissue around each cell. The body's defence system (lymph system) tries to remove the infection caused by abnormal growth. That helps spread the cancer through the lymph system and down through the liver as small cells migrate through the blood supply or lymph drainage and lodge into other parts of the body.

In a language you are going to learn rapidly as your doctor discusses the cancer with you, a primary cancer is where the cancer originally started. Where the little cells spread and start to grow, that is called a secondary cancer. If a cell goes into the liver and starts growing there, although it is a liver cancer, it is actually called a secondary breast cancer because it spread from the tumour in the breast.

Doctors are usually very interested in whether or not the cells show up in the lymph system, so they remove either all of the lymph nodes or the sentinel lymph nodes to see if they show signs of cells. The more the cancer has spread, the worse the prognosis, and the more aggressive (on average) the treatment.

It is my understanding that it takes approximately 30 lots of doubling of cancer cells before they are big enough to be become detectable (30 doublings is approximately the size of a match head). However, if the growth rate continues at a perfect rate (it depends upon the blood supply in the body) then, by the time 40 doublings have occurred, the cancer is a large mass of approximately the size of a small lemon. Therefore, your cancer was growing long before a lump was found. It also means that cells may be circulating in your body but are not yet detectable.

Surgery is often used to remove the primary cancer, but there is the potential for cells to remain in the body. Because a lot of these cells are not able to be detected (for example, through blood tests), the period of time following surgical treatment is a waiting game. The cells need to have 30-odd doublings before they will be detectable. For many types of cancers, that is why the first 5 years following an initial diagnosis become so important. This is the period during which the cells are most likely to become detectable.

The treatment for cancer varies, but effectively it revolves around killing or cutting off the growth of fast-growing cells. Treatment such as chemotherapy kills fast-growing cells. That is why a person's hair falls out and the gut feels sick (the hair and gut are also full of fast growing cells). The predominant purpose of chemo is to kill cancer cells throughout the body, wherever they may be located. Therefore, if some cells migrate to the liver, the chemo kills them before they grow to a problematic size.

Radiotherapy uses radiation to try to kill cells in a local area. That is, the cells which have infused or migrated near to the original tumour, either through margins (edge) of the tumour or the local lymph or other systems. Importantly, it aims to get those cells missed during surgery. However, it is a local area treatment and can cause damage to good tissue and bone in the same area.

The third type of treatments cut off some of the source of growth which allows cells to multiply. For example, anti-hormone treatments for cancers either stop the hormones being produced in the body so the cancer has nothing to grow on, or block the receptors in the cells so the cells cannot absorb the hormone.

Different treatments suit women of different ages, and different cancer types and severity. Therefore, an oncologist is the specialist who can advise you about the effectiveness of the different treatments relevant to your cancer. Oncologists have charts which allow you to decide between different treatments based on percentages. You will need to listen carefully and collect good information during the appointment with your oncologist so that you can decide which treatment combination will be most appropriate for you.

Action Summary:-

- Cancer is the rapid growth of cells, and treatment either cuts out the cancer, kills growing cells, or inhibits the growth of cells. Treatment is matched to the cancer severity, location and type. This matching of treatment also takes into account your age and other factors. It is important that you get good advice quickly.

- Two of the most important times in the treatment process are: meeting with the surgeon if surgery is indicated, and discussing treatments with the oncologist. Make sure that you take notes and/or bring a friend to ensure that you capture as much information as possible.

MEDICAL SPECIALISTS

There are some things you need to know about medical specialists, otherwise the system is going to shock and overwhelm you. The first point to realise is that oncologists and surgeons deal with cancer day in, day out. This may be your only experience with cancer, however, you are only one of the specialists' many cases.

I take my hat off to those people who are willing to devote their lives to try and help people with a very serious life-threatening illness. Many of their clients will end up dying because, sadly, the reality is that not all cancer is treatable. Therefore, doctors need their own emotional survival techniques.

I remember the first oncologist my wife went to was able to remember our jokes from appointment to appointment, but on each visit he had to look up the type of cancer my wife had. He was a very bright man. The fact that he could remember us and our humour means that his coping mechanism was to dissociate (distance himself) from the actual illness.

You will find that your specialists have developed

ways to cope with the intensity of the emotions they deal with. Some of this may be through: intellectualisation (you will feel like a piece of meat being examined, and be presented with cold hard facts); burn-out (a specialist who has lost so many patients that they tend to take a very negative view and could be quite cynical with you); or authoritarian (some doctors will take the 'doctor knows best' approach because they get sick of people coming up with hair-brained situations, or they may even tell you to "*toughen up*" – as one surgeon told my wife).

If you want to survive your medical practitioner's approach, my advice is to use logic which allows you to see the practitioner's benefits but avoids their limitations. You will see a specialist for medical advice, not necessarily for empathy and understanding. Any empathy and understanding you receive is a bonus. What you want is state-of-the-art treatment, accurate knowledge and time to be able to explain yourself. If your doctor can give you those, then you have a good doctor. If your doctor is understanding and empathetic, that is icing on the cake. Do not specifically seek understanding and empathy in your doctor – seek it elsewhere.

Having said that, I recommend that you work with specialists who can at least give you time and are willing to assist you in difficult situations. For example, my wife's second oncologist was willing for me to email her with my concerns. She was a woman of few words, but a couple of thoughtful sentences in an email helped to relieve my concerns.

The bottom line is that the doctors are also trying to survive, so do not take their survival strategies personally.

Action Summary:-

- Working with people with cancer is a very draining process for doctors and other medical staff. Therefore your specialists are coping with their experiences just like you are. It is imperative that you do not allow their emotional issues to cloud your treatment. Set your expectations at a low level in regards to the amount of emotional support you receive from specialists. You are paying them to look after your cancer treatment and your body. Anything they do which helps your heart and mind is a bonus.

- If you want empathy, see a psychologist or attend a cancer group. However, that does not mean that you should not stand up to (or change) a doctor who is rude or disrespectful.

- It is important that you look for good knowledge and service from someone you can trust.

Medical Specialists

Ask around for recommendations for good doctors or specialists in their field. If you know any chemotherapy nurses, they can be very helpful in suggesting who may be a considerate doctor.

DECISIONS IN A CRISIS

When you see your doctor you are going to be presented with a myriad of choices about treatment options. You therefore have to make decisions in a crisis situation.

As explained earlier, in a crisis the limbic system (emotional system) is highly active and the cortex (thinking system) is low. Therefore, decision-making becomes a very difficult process. It is possible that, at a time when decisions were never more critical, you are now least able to make those decisions. We also spoke about the grief overlay and denial as a common first stage of grief. Therefore, you may not want to see the need for treatment when time is of the essence.

So, how can you get through this grief situation? Well, my advice is to ensure you collect facts and, in particular, make notes of those facts. My wife and I are logical people, and we therefore asked lots of questions about probabilities. For each of the main breast cancer treatment options (surgery, radiation and anti-hormone treatment), there are elaborate tables of survival rates. The first time we went through the treatment options, as a younger woman my wife's survival rate with chemotherapy improved by 35%, however, radiation treatment would only add a few percent more. The side effects from radiation, in her mind, were not worth the extra couple of percent. However, when we went through the treatment options a second time, both chemotherapy and radiation had only a modest improvement in survival rate. Therefore, the second time she chose to have both treatments. The weight you put on the survival rate percentages is entirely up to you – even a few percent gain may be significant enough for one person to consider treatment that another person would not do.

In addition to choosing a treatment based on probability, the emotional impact of the treatment choices is also important. After her first chemotherapy treatment, my wife vowed that she would not have chemotherapy a second time. However, we were blessed with the miracle of having boy / girl twins after that first chemotherapy (a near medical impossibility). Therefore, the fact that she had two 10 year old children changed the weight she placed on chemotherapy as a treatment option, so she chose to have it again.

There is no single method for weighing up the variables. However, unless you have the facts and some idea of the implications of each choice, it is very hard to make sensible decisions.

It is also important that you prioritise the different decisions to be made. There are some decisions that need to be made right away, while other decisions can be left until later. Cancer grows. Small delays in treatment do not always make a lot of difference, but long delays can allow the cancer to spread and become more difficult to treat.

My final advice is to make the best decision possible with the information you have – walk forward and do not look back. If you decide not to have radiation treatment, and a local secondary cancer forms, you cannot go back to that choice and relive it. Make new choices based on the current evidence.

Action Summary:-

- Facts are your friends. Get as many facts as possible from your specialist. These facts need to include the benefits in terms of survival if you have the treatment, the impact if you do not have it, the side effects from the treatment, any long-term complications, and any short-term problems from the treatment. The treatments are often brutal, but it is important to know what you are dealing with.

- It is also important to ask about timeframes. It may be that you have to decide on chemotherapy immediately, but a decision whether or not to have radiation treatment can be made later (or vice versa).

- Facts do not make decisions. People make decisions. You are an emotional being and your decision will be impacted by both the logical and the emotional weight of that decision. This where the early sections of this book matter – in which stage of grief are you and how is that impacting upon the decisions you make?

- Look forward and not back. Make the best decision you can at the time. Make a note in a journal so that later on you can recall the basis for that decision.

INFORMATION OVERLOAD

In the previous chapter I explained that facts are good. I would go so far as to say that facts are fantastic. Unfortunately, we live in a world in which our fact-collecting capacity is unlike anything previously experienced in history. I am, of course, talking about the Internet's capacity to access information.

When you go online to search for information, there is a myriad of information on cancer. This information ranges from the conspiracy theories I have referred to previously, outlines of services or treatments offered by various hospitals and clinics, through to research in scholarly journals.

I am a psychologist and an academic. As a professor I am therefore used to reading journal articles. I used to look up some of the cancer studies on the Internet and I would from time to time run the more exciting content past my wife's oncologist. She would then say *"Well, that study does not apply because there is a difference in the type of cancer (subjects, treatment etc.)"*. A study can seem plausible to an outside observer, however, it could describe something entirely different to an expert. Therefore, be very careful about over-interpreting information which is outside of your knowledge base.

In addition, it is very easy to get information overload from the Internet. It is better to do your research on specific issues at each point in time, and do not invest too much time looking too widely. One of the benefits of having a specialist is that they have read and integrated the literature into their working knowledge. Specialists also attend conferences where they hear about ideas not yet reported in the literature (as it might take several years for research to be reported in a journal article).

However, I strongly encourage anyone in a crisis situation to obtain information because it gives you a sense of control. Therefore, the compelling desire to look up information is a basic human driver, that is, to be in control so that you can make decisions. It is ultimately a need to be in control of your body and your life. As long as you understand that the need for control is a part of the process, then you will be able to be selective about the information you rely upon.

Action Summary:-

- Facts are your fantastic friends! However, the more friends you have the more there are disputes between their various interests. Be careful about collecting too much information on cancer and treatments as it can be misleading.

- It is helpful to run ideas past specialists as they will quickly tell you whether or not you are on to something helpful or if it should be discounted. It is hard to judge medical research on the basis of single pieces of information. To complicate things further, the media often portrays breakthroughs in cancer as game changers, when they may be only slight improvements or have no practical benefit yet.

- The Internet provides information. You have to decide what to do with the information you find, because you can find massive amounts of it.

- Remember that attempting to control the uncontrollable is a common emotional reason for looking up information. Are you collecting facts to make a decision, or seeking a magical answer to escape the fear?

POSITIVE ATTITUDE

You will hear a lot about the need to have a positive attitude. Some cancer research showed that women with breast cancer who had positive attitudes had a much higher survival rate. However, when an attempt was made to reproduce the results of that study, it was not possible to do so.

Studies in other areas (such as heart attacks) have often shown that people with positive attitudes recover more quickly and have better survival rates. Therefore, there appears to be some correlation between a positive attitude and improved survival rates.

A more significant finding arising from research into positive attitudes in all aspects of psychological and health functioning, is that those people with positive attitudes have a higher quality of life. Therefore, finding ways to be positive may or may not help you to live longer or overcome your cancer, but it will ensure that the experience you have will be better for you and those around you.

There are a number of psychological strategies which can assist you to be more positive, such as mindfulness. The essence of mindfulness is that you are able to enjoy the moment and remain connected with current experiences. This certainly has some merit. There are courses in mindfulness and some therapists teach mindfulness strategies. A book search will quickly reveal many titles on this topic.

A second strand to positiveness concerns the content of your thinking processes. If you control your thoughts you can be more positive. Psychology calls it Cognitive Behavioural Therapy (CBT). Those people who learn to think in the positive are more robust and less likely to suffer from depression and anxiety. There is good research to show that positive thinking is a skill which can be learnt.

Meditation and relaxation have also been shown to have benefit to the functioning of the body. They help to lower stress levels. It is also well-documented that a lower stress level improves the body's immune system. Therefore, it is important for you to find ways to lower your stress levels and maximise your positivity. Mediation, relaxation, self-hypnosis, guide imagery, yoga, tai chi and related techniques are commonly used to lower stress levels. They are also good for mental health and may improve your physical health as well.

There are self-help books, treatment groups, support groups and other types of information available on all of these techniques. Some of these options are discussed in more detail below.

Action Summary:-

- The mind-body connection is well documented. Ensure that you look after your mental health by developing a positive attitude. Learning stress reduction and relaxation techniques will also help you. Some of the mind-body techniques may also help to cure some types of cancer and relieve treatment side effects. More importantly, good mental health can without exception improve your quality of life.

- Attitude can be learnt and a positive attitude has been shown to be a protective factor in mental health. However, the strong negative emotions associated with cancer have a huge impact on your ability to keep a positive attitude. It is important to build up positive mental health skills, either through self-study or professional input.

TALKING TO PEOPLE

It is more difficult to fight cancer on your own. However, in some respects no one else can experience your journey. People who have had cancer may have had similar journeys to yours, however, their journey will never be exactly the same. Nonetheless, sharing your journey with others can be beneficial. The benefit to sharing is that it helps to keep you mentally healthy.

People are more willing to listen during the early stages of your experience. As time goes on, you may find that some people will get impatient with you and want you to move on or get over it. Therefore, be aware that the usefulness of talking to some people will change over time.

In my opinion, finding someone you can talk to about your experiences is essential. As described earlier, it is possible to compartmentalise with different people the various aspects of your experience. These people may be family, friends or professionals.

Talking to family can often be the most difficult, because they are invested in the outcome. They do not want to see their sister, aunty or mother having doubts, anxieties or fears. Consequently, they may not want to hear some of the things you most need to talk about. You may not want to share some things with them as you have always been the strong one and/or the emotional caretaker of the family.

Talking to friends can be really beneficial if you have good friends who understand you. Some friends may try to tell you to *"just think positively"* or they may want to tell you about treatment strategies. What matters is that you find someone who you believe will listen to you. It is about being understood. When that does not happen, you may be in a lonely place.

On average, women find it easier to talk to others than men do. Men are therefore probably more likely to need to talk to others. It is important that if you have a spouse or partner going through this experience (or going through it with you), that they find someone with whom they can offload. In many relationships the wife is often the main or only person in whom the husband confides, so it can be a problem when you have your own overload of emotion. It will be very hard for him to talk to you about his fears for you, and you may not be in a place to hear it. Therefore it is important that your partner also gets support.

Seeing a professional person, a therapist or counsellor can be very beneficial for your quality of life. They can be an independent person for you to talk to. However, it is important that you have a counsellor or therapist that you can relate to – somebody with whom you feel comfortable and who has a good knowledge base. In some parts of the world, such as Australia, anyone can be a counsellor but psychologists are registered. Therefore, you have to look very carefully at the advice you receive if the person you consult is not properly trained.

There are a number of different support groups for cancer sufferers. Some people really enjoy going to a support group where they are surrounded by like-minded people, sharing a common experience. In your daily life you may feel separate and isolated, but going to a group will help you to share the experience with other people who are having the same problems.

The downside of attending a group is that you are surrounded by sick people whose issues may well trigger your own. Therefore, I recommend experimenting with groups to see whether it works for or against you. If it works for you, enjoy it. If it works against you, then get those needs met through other means.

Being different can be incredibly personal. During

her cancer, my wife became close to her three sisters due to the common fear of getting breast cancer. My wife then discovered that she had a gene for cancer and that her sisters could be tested. Luckily for all three sisters, none had the gene. Suddenly my wife was alone as the sisters no longer shared that common bond with her.

Action Summary:-

- Talking is good as long as the person "*gets*" you. Finding people who understand you can be difficult. However, it is essential that you find some outlets for your emotion.

- If you have a partner, you need to keep the lines of communication open otherwise, over time, your relationship will unravel. The tricky part is finding a balance between addressing your inner fears and overwhelming your partner.

- A partner often feels powerless as they have to watch what is happening and cannot do anything. Men find it hard to talk at the best of times so it will be even harder when it involves their fears for you. If you are not in a relationship, or you have an alternative relationship, there are some key issues in dealing with your partner's emotions and feelings.

- Consider support groups. Good or fantastic for some, and depressing or overwhelming for others. If it works, go for it. If not, realise that it causes triggers for you and do something different. There is no right way to do things but it is important to experiment.

TRAUMA

An important aspect to be aware of is the difference between emotion and trauma. Emotion makes us human. Common emotions are happiness, sadness and frustration. The brain is designed to remember those things which are particularly good and bad. We want to remember the good things to seek more pleasure, and avoid the bad to so as not to get hurt again. The brain is particularly good at both. Without these things life would be like a dull void. There has to be opposition in all things to better understand experiences. Without pain, you would not realise what pleasure is.

As discussed earlier, flight, fight and freeze systems are activated at the start of a crisis. It is normal to feel these emotions. They may overwhelm you (often in waves or surges of feelings), but they prevent the build-up of pressure. In psychology, if you experience the emotions you are more likely to have underlying processes. However, the system can overload if the negative experiences are too strong or go on for too long. The overload happens when the brain cannot process the emotions and the bad memories keep replaying. Therefore, sadness becomes depression and frustration becomes anger. These are problematic emotions, not normal or healthy emotions.

If something (such as hearing a comment about cancer on television) causes you to feel upset for a while but you settle afterwards, that reaction is pretty normal. Without the trigger, if your brain is full of memories of what you have been through, or if a trigger causes you to keep thinking of the negative experiences, then you may have fallen into trauma. Post-Traumatic Stress Disorder (PTSD) occurs when the brain is full of flashbacks and terrible memories. The symptoms fall into two broad domains, namely, the arousal domain (recurrent thoughts, sleeplessness, irritability or anxiousness) and the avoidance domain (feeling depressed, disconnected or dissociated).

If you experience these symptoms then it indicates that you need help to get your emotions back in balance. The evidence says that the more you face the trauma, the more likely you are to get over it (that is, if you avoid a fear or feeling, it stays the same or gets worse). There are some particularly helpful therapy techniques such as Eye Movement Desensitisation and Reprocessing (EMDR), which a professional such as a psychologist can use to help you.

Action Summary:-

- After a trigger, if you have excessive emotions and they pass quickly, then that is a normal experience.

- If you have excessive emotions from small triggers (or no triggers), or if you are overwhelmed with heavy emotions (such as anger, depression and despair), which linger for several weeks or more, then you may have moved from a normal reaction into trauma. It is important that you seek help from trained professionals.

SURVIVING TREATMENT

Chemotherapy and radiation are treatment regimens which, due to variations in the disease and the person, will be different for different people. For breast cancer, chemotherapy is often delivered on a 3-weekly basis in 6 cycles. The chemotherapy drugs may change after some of these cycles. Radiation treatment is delivered on a daily basis for 6 weeks. This may vary depending upon the type of treatment you have.

The net result is that the chemicals will be in your body over a reasonable period of time in order to maximise the opportunity to kill fast-growing cells. Therefore, if you have 4-6 months of treatment, it is a fairly long period to have to get through.

While everyone is different, and the delivery of the treatment varies considerably for each individual, these treatments can be brutal. When science finally unlocks the mysteries to controlling cell division, cancer treatments will change (for example, where drugs are targeted at cancer cells). Once that is in place, future doctors will look back at our current treatment regimens with horror! Until that day, these treatments are the best we have. The treatment is tough, so prepare yourself.

There are a number of things you can do to help get through the situation. One strategy is to set a long-term goal aimed at the end of treatment. For example, my wife had always wanted to see polar bears. Some insurance money associated with her cancer diagnosis provided us with the money for a trip to Canada. This was planned for a period of time after her recovery, but it meant that we could focus on a positive future event through the dark times.

A second strategy we employed through the current round of radiation treatment was what we called 'micro holidays'. This was as simple as spending a single night in a hotel, or taking a weekend trip to a different part of Australia. The idea behind it was to break up the block of treatment with small escapes. While it may not seem much, the couple of nights we spent in Alice Springs in the middle of radiation made a tremendous difference to being able to get through the relentless nature of the daily treatment. We planned these trips over a radiation machine service day, which allowed us to effectively have 3 nights away.

Note, however, that if your planned activities involve flying, will your immune system allow you to fly and, if travelling overseas, will you be able to find travel insurance to cover you if you experience complications? These are practical matters which are important to discuss with doctors and your insurance company. Nothing would be worse than needing complicated medical treatment overseas, which might not be covered by your insurance (but would have been covered if you had been at home).

It will help if you get as fit as you can prior to starting treatment, and then keep fit for all of the rigours of the processes which you will go through. I fully accept that going through treatments such as chemotherapy, radiation and surgery takes a tremendous toll on the body. Under those circumstances you are certainly not going to be performing as an elite athlete. You will also become less and less able to keep fit as each cycle of treatment occurs. However, there are several really important reasons why trying to stay fit is beneficial.

We know that from an emotional point of view physical exercise has positive benefits in relation to depression and anxiety. Therefore, whether you take a walk, jog, ride a bike, swim or do something else, exercise helps to lower stress and improve your outlook. Importantly, the fitter you are the better you will recover from surgery and bounce back from other treatments.

Fatigue commonly occurs with these types of

treatment. While being exhausted makes it very difficult to do anything physical, small amounts of exercise can help you to overcome the fatigue. Therefore, do what you can to keep moving and keep as fit as possible. Ensure that any exercise is only commenced with the approval of your doctors, particularly if you have had surgery or are taking medications which can interfere with your heart and other organs.

It is equally important to consider practical matters, such as attending appointments. At first you may be well enough to drive but over time you may not be able to do so. You may be taking medications which interfere with your capacity to drive safely. More importantly, having someone to support you during treatment is essential. My wife and I used to joke that the reason you have someone drive you to chemotherapy is that if you drove yourself you would not stop at the hospital!

If you have a support person, make sure that your supporter is what you need. My wife and I organised a roster of drivers to take her to radiation so that she did not have to drive. However, after a few weeks we realised that she needed an emotional support person and not a driver. We then had to get a different set of people involved who were capable of (and compatible with) being emotionally supportive.

Action Summary:-

- Chemotherapy is never pleasant and is often a vile treatment. Make a plan for the future after the treatment (and you have had a few months to recover). Future after planning can keep you out of the day-to-day horrors associated with the treatment.

- Micro holidays or other opportunities to get away are useful in enabling you to regroup your feelings, instead of focussing completely on the treatment.

- Do not compare yourself to other people having treatment, as some people barely miss a beat while others may experience rare and unusual side effects.

- Get as fit as possible before treatment and try to keep the exercise going during and after treatment. However, make sure that you do it with medical advice.

- Acknowledge that you do not need to do this alone. Get help when you need it. I caution you to pick your support people wisely.

CHEMOTHERAPY HORRORS

When you have chemotherapy, the oncologist will provide you with a summary of some of the impacts, side effects and other factors associated with the treatment. However, this might not capture the degree with which it is going to impact upon you.

The first thing to consider is that people vary widely. There are some people who are very sick from the first dose, while other people breeze through the whole process. What I do know, however, is that the effects tend to be cumulative. Therefore, the first dose is often the easiest. By the time the last dose is administered you will reach your highest levels of fatigue. You cannot make your decisions based upon the way you coped with the first round of treatment.

Fatigue may continue after the treatment ends. Therefore, plan on the basis that you will get progressively worse, and do not use the first treatment as a measure of the entire process. Tired is normal. You may want to know whether you will be able to keep working. That is a good question, but largely impossible to answer until the treatment starts and you can see what is involved.

Your specialists can help you to manage the side-effects of chemotherapy. In the fifteen years between my wife's first and second treatments, the treatment itself had only progressed a little but the management of the side effects was extremely different. You no longer have to suffer many of the side effects – there are often drugs to help. The key point is that you have to raise your concerns with the doctors. To do so is not being a nuisance, but acting on your rights.

I also think that it is important to work out whether there is a predictable pattern to the way in which the treatment affects you. The first time we went through chemotherapy they used to give my wife steroids and anti-nausea medications in a large dose at the time of the initial treatment (it is done differently now). Therefore, on the first day of treatment she would be on a hunger high. We would often go out for a nice meal together. Several days after that, she would collapse in a heap and not want to eat again. However, we enjoyed brief moments of pleasure in an otherwise bleak scenario. The second time around, the steroids were lower and she did not experience the same problems with eating.

Psychologists have been researching *"chemo brain"* effects. It has been well-documented that for some people chemotherapy interferes with short-term memory and other types of thinking processes. The research is still out in terms of trying to predict who this will affect and how – while all people are affected, not all people are affected equally. A number of people will find that they have short-term memory problems, confusion and so forth.

Accept that your memory will not be as good, so use reminders. In my opinion, you should treat this situation much like you would treat any form of short-term memory condition, and that is to ensure that you take notes, do not rely on memory, and keep records of as many things as possible. Neuropsychologists are not sure how much of the impact is long-term, but the research shows that everyone improves in the first two years after treatment.

There is no doubt that chemotherapy has an impact upon your immune system. The specialists will do all they can to monitor and improve your body's systems to build up your health. The psychology of this is two part. There is some limited evidence that relaxation and visualisation can help improve immune response. The second and perhaps the most important part is that you need to keep away from other people when the doctors tell you to. Being near sick people when you have a compromised immune system could land you in hospital or even kill you.

It is tough to avoid family functions because of cancer, but do not risk it. If there is a very special event, like a family wedding, advise your specialists so that they can time your treatment around the event to maximise your immunity.

Action Summary:-

- Chemotherapy and radiation are treatments which side-effects that become progressively worse. Do not judge how you are going by the way you feel after the first cycle. It tends to get worse over time.

- Speak up about side effects. Many side effects can be managed, but unless you tell your doctor or nurses they will not be alert to what you need. Being stoic is only admirable to a point.

- If you can work out a pattern of how the chemo affects you, try to grab the moments during which you are feeling better to do good things. Plan to write off those days when you are at your worst.

- "*Chemo brain*" has been shown to exist. Your memory will not be same during and immediately after treatment. It will improve but, until it does, use reminders and do not rely on memory alone.

- Keep safe. People may think you are being "selfish" for not attending family or other functions, however, attending such functions can be life-threatening during treatment. Do not risk it.

LOSING HAIR AND OTHER LOSSES

The most humiliating aspects for those people who have to undergo cancer treatment is both the private losses through surgery (surgery to, or removal of, breasts), and the publicly visible effects of cancer or cancer treatment. In no area is the public face of cancer more evident than the loss of hair from chemotherapy.

There are a few important things to know about hair loss, which are often not clear from talking to a specialist. The first is that hair loss is a predictable side effect of certain types of chemotherapy. Therefore, your specialist will be able to tell you not only if you will lose your hair, but approximately when that will happen. Sometimes it is after the first or second treatment.

Because chemotherapy kills fast-growing cells, all of the hair cells are killed simultaneously (meaning that the hair falls out pretty well all at once). In this process the hair begins to moult and then comes out primarily in tufts. One day the hair is there, and within a few days you will look quite threadbare. Denial often prevents you from acting earlier, so when it happens it is too late to take any preparatory action.

There are a few things that can be of assistance in this process. First of all, think about family photos. After the first dose of chemo it may be 3-6 weeks before the loss of hair occurs. It may be possible to organise family photos while you still have hair, but do not delay (better still, organise this before treatment).

Once your hair starts to grow back (after the particular type of chemotherapy has finished), your hair will grow back about 1cm a month. Therefore, it is usually around 4-6 months after the end of the treatment that your hair will begin to get to a length where it can be cut again. The hair may also grow back frizzy or a different colour, which can change after 12 months (unless you are one of the unfortunate people who ends up with a different look after treatment). In other words, you will not look normal again until after a year.

In anticipation of losing your hair there are a few things you can do to help. First of all, if you have long hair cut it short prior to the chemotherapy. That way, it is not such a drastic change of appearance – it becomes a two-stage change. Denial often pokes its head up on this issue, *"maybe I won't lose my hair"*.

One of the things my wife did when her hair was starting to fall out, was to use clippers to take the hair off. The kids thought it was quite funny to be a part of the process. It stopped them from being so scared about it. It also gave my wife some degree of control in the sense that she was cutting her hair off rather than waiting for it to fall out. It was still a sad day, but not as bad as if her hair had just fallen out.

An American friend had some little boxes in which she placed and then buried her hair (this ritual was based around a native American tradition). It was like having a mini-funeral for her hair. This allowed her to both grieve and have some control.

As with the theme of my book, it is not necessary for you to do what we have done, but you should think about how you can do it your way. Doing things which allow you to have some control (e.g. cutting your hair off yourself), or things which allow you to face your fear in bite-sized chunks. These are things that are going to be beneficial to you, whereas those people who passively wait have greater problems.

Once your hair has gone you need to find a way of dealing with the situation. Some people like wigs. Others find wigs hot and uncomfortable. Before your hair goes it is important to buy some hats and other types of head coverings for you to use.

It is also important to realise that it is not just hair on the head, but all body hair will go (including eyebrows, eyelashes and pubic hair). Fortunately, eyelashes and eyebrows tend to grow back quite quickly after the chemo ceases, however, considering some alternatives may be beneficial if looks are important to you.

Action Summary:-

- If the chemotherapy results in the loss of your hair, expect it to come out all at once. Hope or denial may stop you from taking action early. When the hair loss happens it will be a shock.

- Think practical. Get the family photos done before chemo starts (or very soon after the first dose) or you may not get another chance for a year.

- If you have long hair, consider getting it cut short so that the change is not as drastic when it happens.

- *Are there things you can do when your hair falls out which help you to either grieve the loss or have control of the process?* Cutting it yourself, involving the children, burying the hair in a ceremony or anything else which feels right for you to do.

- Wigs, hats or scarves are a personal choice. It does not matter what you choose, but it does help to get in early so you are prepared.

BREASTS

Breasts are one of the most defining features of womanhood. They are what mark the onset of womanhood. They are intimately involved in sexuality and an integral part of nurturing babies for many women. In effect, they are a very intimate and personal part of a woman's being.

Breast cancer is unlike cancer in almost any other part of the body because of the breast's strong association with identity and womanhood. It is not just a body part but part of an identity. Therefore, there are reactions to breast cancer which are greater than for some other types of cancer. Not only will there be grief in relation to the cancer, there may also be grief in relation to the breasts themselves.

In the simplest experiences of breast cancer, treatment might involve a lumpectomy. This can have an impact at an identity level. However, breast removal can be profound in its impact. Like all things, there are a variety of reactions. Some aspects are discussed below.

After surgery, you might feel relief that the cancer

is gone. It is a good thing to get rid of the cancer. In many respects the best treatment for cancer is removal. Once it is gone there are no cancer cells to grow (but the doctors might not know if they have removed all of the cells). Doctors will be especially pleased to explain that the tests showed no cells in the surgery margins and that the cancer is gone. Apart from this relief, the impacts are more emotional and profound.

Loss of something results in grief. Loss of a breast can include grief which impacts at the level of identity. It can leave some women feeling that their femininity has been damaged. When there has been no breast reconstruction, waking up after a mastectomy and seeing the result for the first time can be devastating. The complete absence of the breast may trigger a myriad of emotions. It will take time to get used to the change and I think that no one comes to terms with it completely. The best to hope for is acceptance.

An option for some women is that they have a reconstruction after the mastectomy. This entails building a new breast to replace the old one. Whether at the time, or sometime later, there is some comfort in having a shape which looks a bit like a breast. It is also preferable to wake up from the anaesthetic seeing a breast shape (but reconstruction is a gruelling process).

Unfortunately, when the surgeons discuss breast surgery and reconstructions they can create a hope that the breast will be replaced. *"New boobies for Christmas"* seems to be the promise. However, surgery damages most of the nerve pathways so not much feeling remains. Sadly, it does not look the same, nor does it feel the same. Many women may be disappointed that reconstruction did not give them their breast back.

I read an article by cosmetic tattooist who specialised in drawing nipples on reconstructed breasts. She said that many women are quite traumatised by the time they have this procedure. Up to that point they have been in crisis mode and have not had a chance to process the experience. The reconstruction and nipples are the last part of the process and it may be the first time the woman has been able to stop and reflect on the journey. The loss may be profound as you realise that the treatment is over but you did not get your breasts back.

When considering reconstruction, note that radiation toughens the skin. Therefore you need to make enquiries about the timing of radiation and the reconstruction. You need to have options, so get the facts early.

My wife had a mastectomy surgery on one breast, and the psychological impact was not too bad.

However, when the second breast was removed, the impact was much more significant for both of us. It had a significant impact when it happened, and in some respects was more profound than grief (it would be best described as trauma).

Women who have beast-fed babies may feel disloyal to the part of their body that nurtured their babies. Losing the breast which fed the baby can result in feelings of profound loss or disloyalty to the breast itself. When a younger woman has breast cancer before having children, the loss of the breast can be notable (a later section of this book discusses whether to farm your eggs to use after treatment).

On another level, breasts are generally a part of sexuality and intimacy in a relationship. A loss of breasts can impact upon the feelings of being sexual, the desire for sexual activity, and the level of responsiveness achieved. It is important to consider and address these issues as they arise. However, for all the jokes about sex, sexual matters are difficult to talk about to others (but if you don't talk no one can help you).

A husband or partner may also feel significant grief at the loss of "*our*" breasts. These are normal feelings which need to be addressed by having open communication and, if necessary, professional assistance. I can only stress that the loss of her breasts can have a profound impact upon a woman.

Action Summary:-

- Breasts are an intimate part of a woman's being and there is grief involved in the loss of breasts through surgery. Each woman is different, but it is important to understand that the impact can be profound for many women.

- Reconstruction offers some relief as the breasts still look like breasts under clothing. However, the breasts will not be same and even the best surgery in the world cannot replace what you have lost. It is normal, healthy and appropriate to grieve this loss.

- Sexuality in the relationship will be affected by the sickness resulting from treatment, but the loss of a breast can have an impact upon your relationship to very core levels. Sexuality is one of the hardest topics to discuss in many relationships, yet it is essential to have open communication. Professional assistance is sometimes needed to help with grief, for your partner or both of you.

MAKE YOUR PEACE

A cancer diagnosis forces you to look death in the eye. You are mortal, and at some point you are going to die. Cancer brings it home that this could be sooner rather than later.

This dark fact is something that most people want to avoid facing, which is why denial and avoidance strategies are so predominant when people are diagnosed with cancer. Whether or not you talk about it, it lurks in the back of your mind under these circumstances.

The point I would like to make is that we do have a limited window of time upon this earth. It is important, especially if you have been diagnosed with cancer, to do something about your life. The first is to do a stock-take and decide if you are living the sort of life you want to live. I am not saying that now is the time to have a complete sea change, especially in the middle of a medical crisis, however, it is important to weigh up how you spend your time.

If you have disputes within your family, or in your life, you should not let those disputes linger. Now is the time to make your peace so that you have no regrets. In a lot of ways *"no regrets"* should be your motto through this part of your life. The decisions you make, and the things you do, should be the best possible choices you could make, with no regrets. If there are things you regret from the past, see what you can do to fix them.

If the news becomes increasingly bleak, or the cancer becomes terminal, it is important to ensure that you consider the impact on your family. I know when my mother-in-law died she wrote a letter to all of the members of her choir, but could not face writing the same letter to her children. I believe that this has had a quite profound impact upon her children. Therefore, whether you make video clips for special events in the children's lives, or simply write letters or notes, it can be very beneficial to express your feelings, love and wishes at different points in the lives of your family.

If you have younger children, one of your greatest fears while you are going through this cancer process is what will happen to your children. While you may not want to face it from your point of view, having worked with children who have suffered grief and loss I know that children who have some concrete evidence of their parent's love for them do better than those who do not have that evidence.

I know faith can bring a lot of comfort to those who have it. I believe in a loving Heavenly Father who knows what is happening in even the darkest of times. However, the purpose of life is faith. We have to travel through life by our faith and not rely upon God to fix things for us. If left to decide who should or should not die, mortals would never allow anyone to pass from this world. I also know that even believing in God means that, during difficult times, we will have a trial of our faith. Therefore, make sure that you get spiritual help and guidance as you move through these difficult times.

Action Summary:-

- Talk of dying is a grim topic which most people avoid. However, cancer has caused you to face this fact. It is important that you recognise everyone only has a limited time, and cancer has made this more significant for you. It is okay to feel fear, anxiety and stress at the prospect of this thought. It is what you do with these feelings which matters.

- Are you living the life you want? The time to make major changes should not be during medical treatment, but it is important that you evaluate your priorities in life. If you need to have a sea-change then start planning for it when you are well.

- "No regrets" should be your motto from now on. Clear past baggage and get your life in order.

- If it is appropriate for you, leave a legacy for your children. Videos, letters and other communications can be quite important in children's lives, even adult children.

- Spirituality and religion offer comfort in difficult times, however, every aspect of your belief may be challenged during cancer.

THE PRACTICAL

There are a number of practical things one can do when faced with cancer. The first is an expression I heard about someone who had a near death experience, where they said that afterwards they *"chose to travel lighter"*. What they meant by this was they got rid of a lot of their material and emotional baggage. In the home they simplified their life so that they could literally travel lighter in material ways. However, they also meant this in a psychological way. They let go of their life baggage too.

As we go through life we work on the assumption that we will live forever. Having a cancer diagnosis should be a wake-up call for you to get your affairs in order. Hopefully you will not need it, but it will be a big relief to know that you have a current Will and that your insurance policies have been identified and are up-to-date.

Often there are very large worries about small matters. You may express a desire for what should happen to everything from the children to the dog. Having a plan for each of these will be important.

I also think that we clutter our lives with many belongings. Going through the house and cupboards to get rid of junk and put things in order is a big favour for your family (should your outcome worsen). It is also nice to feel in control of something – rearranging a cupboard can help to do this.

There are some people who have their affairs in order to create an easier time for their family. The trouble with having to do this is that you have to face the fact that your own mortality is at stake.

Action Summary:-

- Travel lighter. Simplify your life both emotionally and practically.

- Have you got your affairs in order? Do you have a will? Is your insurance up to date? What else needs to be addressed? It may seem negative or morbid, but there is also comfort in knowing that things are in order.

- Do you have any junk and clutter which you need to get rid of?

IT'S BACK!

The first time through cancer treatment, as hard as it may be, leaves you with an energizing sense of hope. While cancer is incredibly scary, the thought that you may be able to beat this disease is the main driver as you go through the horrendous treatments. In the post-treatment period there may be a sense of relief that you have done everything that you possibly could and the treatment is over. You are going to beat the cancer, and once the treatment is over you feel that you have done well.

At the end of that Herculean effort of survival, people will often ask questions like "are you in remission?" Doctors may even use words like 'remission' and there is a sense of comfort being in the position where there are no current signs of cancer. As explained earlier, however, the small cells multiply until the point where they then become detectable in scans. For many people the cells have been killed and there is no further news (lucky for you if that is the case). Unfortunately, for some people further scans, or self-examination, find a lump. The news, no matter how it is packaged, is that the cancer is back!

Recurrence effectively can be in one of three broad categories. The first is a local tumour where some of the original cells continue to multiply. Second, the cells lodged somewhere else to form a secondary cancer. Third, a new primary cancer is diagnosed elsewhere in the body.

From a treatment perspective, second time diagnosis will bring forward a whole array of treatment issues not apparent in the first round of treatment. There are certain types of chemotherapy that have what is called "lifetime tolerances". A first course of treatment often does not get close to the maximum dose, however, second round treatments will see the oncologists using various formulas to calculate whether the cumulative side effects are going to outweigh the benefit of the standard medications. In some cases the original treatments cannot be fully replicated and other medications will be used in the alternative.

From a psychological perspective second round diagnosis often hits much harder than the initial diagnosis. All the effort the first time was engaged in beating the cancer – the horrendous treatment was to survive the cancer – sadly the tests now show that the cancer was not beaten. There is a sense of powerlessness and hopelessness which were not present the first time (in the initial episode there was hope that it could be beaten). Now it is a like a stalker, lurking in the background ready to strike.

Furthermore, memories of the awful effects of the chemotherapy and other treatments are the new benchmark. The first time through the experience was based on observations of other family members and friends who went through chemotherapy, whereas this time you have your own store of experience to draw from. The worse your experience was during your previous treatment, the greater the possible emotional reaction following re-diagnosis.

Probabilities and odds are typically grimmer on second diagnosis than first diagnosis depending on the circumstances. For example, my wife had had a mastectomy the first time, however, 12 years later the recurrence was on the same side. Consequently, the preventive mastectomy on the other side offers only limited reassurance. Somebody who has had a mastectomy may experience a complete sense of relief that the risk has gone (we know however that the risk is markedly reduced, but not eliminated).

The bottom line is that for many people a second diagnosis (albeit secondary or a new primary) is a much harder, grimmer and psychologically more daunting task to get through. Psychological defences have to work overtime to convince yourself that you can "beat it" this time.

Action Summary:-

- A second diagnosis of cancer is much harder to deal with than the first, as the efforts to beat the disease seem more futile. Depression, anxiety and other feelings can arise.

- Second time around a greater degree of psychological assistance is likely to be necessary, as this is a harder, darker period to work through.

- Be aware that all of the various defence mechanisms discussed earlier may be working overtime.

- At a practical level, try to avoid complacency when attending review appointments – especially if there is some possible adverse finding. Make sure that you have your support person present.

FORGETTING TO LIVE

There is a joke about a man called John lying in bed in a downstairs unit about to go to sleep. The man in the upstairs unit comes home and drops a work boot heavily on the floor. After waiting about half an hour, a frustrated John goes upstairs, knocks on the door and says *"Will you hurry up and drop the other one? I can't sleep."*

Cancer is a lot like that. To some degree, the cancer diagnosis and the treatment that follows forever changes how you view life. You spend your time waiting for the other boot to drop. Another way of putting it is that when you are diagnosed with cancer you hold your breath. As you go through the whole chaotic period of treatment, you continue to hold your breath. Many people who have cancer forget to breathe again. They are waiting for the other boot to drop.

This was brought home to me at a workshop I attended run by John Gottman, a master researcher in the area of family relationships. I was looking at the model he was presenting about the different factors which make a successful relationship.

These factors included communication, conflict resolution, trust and other related dynamics. While he was presenting this, in my mind I was ticking off all of these factors in my own relationship. At the peak of his model was a dynamic called *"shared goals"*. I realised that at the time my wife was diagnosed with cancer we went from having a future life of plans and dreams, to surviving the experience. We had stopped having shared goals because we were in survival mode. Some 10 years later, this workshop made me realise that we had not gone back to having a future, and we were still living on a day-to-day basis.

This is really straightforward to understand. Why live for a future when you may not have one? What is the point in having superannuation if you do not live to share it? Consequently, there is this practical dynamic that cancer causes you to shift from a future focus to a current focus. It is up to you to reconnect with life. The problem is that you cannot have a test to determine whether or not you have cancer (only that there is no evidence of cancer) so there is no point from which to start living again.

As explained earlier, with the little cancer cells growing there is a reasonably large window before you can begin to breathe easily again. The trouble is that by then you are in such a habit of holding your breath that you forget to live. Do make sure that, even if you do not have clear future plans, you can at least decide to do things on a day-by-day or week-by-week basis to have something to look forward to.

It is important that as your treatment finishes you reset your goals. Start initially with a short term goal for 3 or 6 months. Then build back up to goals for future years. It is up to you to learn to live again.

Action Summary:-

- To get through the crisis it is common to hold your breath, waiting for the next crisis. You have to learn to breathe again or you will remain forever waiting for the next episode of cancer or further bad news.

- Survival is about having an immediate focus for today. Survival means that you must deal with the immediate problems. Living is about having a past, present and future. Make sure that you put a future back into your life.

- To get a new future, start by setting little goals. These need only be weeks or months into the future, but later can become years. However, unless you take action you will be in eternal survival mode.

PARTNER'S REACTIONS - SHARED EXPERIENCE

A couple who have been together for years, know each other well, have shared all sorts of adversity with their children and in their life, are confronted with a diagnosis of breast cancer. They are about to go through the same thing – right? Unfortunately, the answer to that is no. Each person will have a different experience.

When cancer is in the family it is not a joint adversity - there are two people having separate experiences. You are coping with a life-threatening illness and issues surrounding your own mortality, and your partner is faced with your possible loss. You may have to have operations, and your partner has to watch. You are going to be sick with the chemotherapy drugs, and your partner has to carry the load. Therefore, this is a different experience with very different realities for each of you. So while the cancer and its difficulties are common to you both, your reactions and coping mechanisms are going to be quite different.

Some of the key dynamics here are that you (who

has the cancer), in an ironic sort of way, have a degree of control in that you can make the decisions about what treatments to have (and then have those treatments). Your partner has no control in that they are passive bystanders to the things which happen to you. Take, for example, when you have surgery you are unconscious to it, while your partner has to wait for the outcome of the surgery. Each of you has a very different experience.

It is very easy for you to take all of the attention and, to some degree, it is completely justified. You are the one experiencing cancer. However, it is important to acknowledge that your partner is also faced with very serious issues, but because their issues are not life-threatening they are sometimes treated as if their issues can be ignored or avoided. It is important that the issues for both of you (and others concerned, such as your children) are addressed.

A second feature in this is that the ways in which people grieve are going to be quite different. As the person who is going through the medical treatment, you are likely to be on a chaotic rollercoaster and not considering things such as whether you will live or die, but how you are going to get through the next treatment. Your partner, on the other hand, may be grieving emotionally about the process and the future.

The situation is further complicated by the fact that men and women tend to grieve differently. Women tend to be more verbal and more emotional. In other words, they talk and cry more about it. Men are more likely to want to do things to help relieve the grief. I remember my father-in-law, when his wife was gravely ill with cancer, dug a sewerage trench by hand. The process of digging was to a certain extent his way of coping with the grief.

It is a further complication that a man's style is often to withdraw at a time when women most need help. Men seek to sort it out themselves and women want to share. Women find their normally cooperative partner is now moody, withdrawn and unavailable.

The implications of this are to recognise that you are each in different places emotionally, and that you are trying to deal with different things. Each person has an important emotional load to deal with, and this needs to be sorted out to prevent damage to your relationship. It is also important to talk about the fact that these issues may be difficult to discuss.

Having said that, it is important that your partner is considerate in the timing of any discussion. It is true they may be fearful that you are going to die, but talking about it just before the operation is not helpful. It is important to get support. Even as a very experienced psychologist, during my wife's second treatment I went to counselling once a month to help me talk through my emotional issues. I was mindful to share with my wife what I spoke about to my therapist, so that my wife could be a part of the process. I did not want her to feel I had pulled away and was no longer sharing with her, but this enabled me to dump my emotions on the counsellor rather than on her.

An example of how a partner should not react is demonstrated by a case I know of where the wife found a breast lump and the husband spent two days in bed! The poor woman went to work while the husband went to pieces. There is something wrong with that picture!

Action Summary:-

- While the cancer is common to both members of a couple, each has a very different experience. Understanding and respecting difference is important. Communication is also important.

- Individuals grieve differently – as do different genders. Women often want to talk or cry. Men want to withdraw and process. Women often get sad. Men often become irritable. It is very different for each of them. Are you aware of how you and your partner are dealing with issues?

- ➤ Relationship counselling or individual therapy are not signs of failure but the marks of someone who wants to survive the psychological pressure of the situation. Why not use the tools which are available?

CHILDREN

There are many aspects to consider about children. There are issues about being able to have children, and issues related to how children cope with their mother having cancer. A few of the key aspects are discussed below.

There is something about the threat of death which triggers the desire for organisms to live. Babies are often conceived after funerals and natural disasters. It is as if a part of your genes wants to go on. However, before rushing into having children, take a reasoned look at your circumstances. It may not be fair on a future child to come into the world if you are not going to be available to parent a child to adulthood. Therefore you need to consider what you can offer a child, not just how a child might fulfil you. Having said that, there are some possibilities to consider.

In younger women chemotherapy often reduces the chance of future fertility to very low levels. Farming eggs prior to chemotherapy may be possible in some cases. There had been a concern that egg farming using stimulating hormones may increase the risk of cancer (as hormones can feed many breast cancers). The evidence now suggests that fertility treatment prior to chemotherapy does not lead to adverse cancer outcomes. However, time is of the essence and many younger women feel rushed to have to decide on the potentially life-changing decision to farm their eggs (so they may forego this so as to not delay treatment). Similarly there may be disappointment if the egg farming is unsuccessful. Therefore, there are complex grief issues surrounding not having children or rushing alternative strategies.

For those of you who still have children at home, there are very real concerns about managing them during the process. My advice is to keep children informed, but to *"drip feed"* the information. Children know when things are wrong. On the day we went to the specialist to get the cancer test results, my son knew the news was bad because he did not ever have play dates after school. He could read the social environment to work out something was wrong. Our best of intentions to keep the news hidden was easily worked out by a 10 year old. Therefore I make sure that they know what is going on in simple factual terms.

I encourage parents to consider telling the truth but delivering it as layers of truth. By this I mean that what you tell your children should be real, but the amount of information should depend upon their age and vary over time. Children will sense if you are dishonest and may later lose trust in you. As I said, drip feeding information over time is also helpful to prevent children from being overwhelmed.

Children can be self-limiting with information. They will ask questions about what they need to know. Then they switch off. Let them ask and they will limit how much you need to tell them.

It is important that they understand there is a risk that the treatment might not work, but deliver that message with a balanced and optimistic spin – *"it is possible that mummy might die, but the treatment is good at fixing these problems"*. Children need optimism and hope.

There are ways to help with the grief a child might experience in the future. I saw one little girl whose mum died of cancer. The girl had been given short video clips of mum talking to her for her 16th birthday, her 18th birthday, her engagement, and her marriage. While this is a very sad thing for the mum to do, it gave this girl some hope and resilience through a very dark time. Mum was there when the girl missed her the most.

Adult children are also disturbed when a parent gets cancer. It is important that they are provided with information. They may also be a good source of support for understanding the information you are given, as they may be more technologically minded.

Action Summary:-

- If you have not had children, then it is important to canvas options (if any) before chemotherapy starts. However, in doing so consider what both the future child and you really want.

- Children are astute. Make sure they are provided with the truth, but in bite-sized and age appropriate doses. They will sense things are going on and it is best they know what is happening.

- Children often ask things but will self-limit the answers. When they know enough they will stop asking questions. Therefore, listen to what your children want to know, rather that telling them every detail.

- Adult children may have problems coping. Make sure that you understand what is going on for them. They can be a useful source of help in a modern world of information. However, you have to go back to my first rule – you must do it your way.

- Consider extra help in the home if there are children. If you have family support, do not be shy in asking your relatives for help. They may like to help as they are feeling powerless. If relatives are not available, au pairs or nannies can be helpful if you can find a good one. Read some material on how to choose a good au pair.

HUMOUR AND WRITING

The first time we went through the cancer experience we created an imaginary book which we nicknamed "*The Black Daffodil*" ('daffodil' being the symbol of cancer, and 'black' because it was so bleak). This was our joke book for going through the cancer experience. One of the ways we used to discharge the fear and anxiety of what we were going through was to make jokes.

To an outsider hearing some of the things we laughed at, you would probably think I was either sick or pathetic. However, in sharing a similar sense of humour, my wife was able to use these experiences to discharge some of the emotion.

Pick up any joke book and it will include all sorts of irreverent subjects, be it life and death or other sorts of things. People also make jokes when there is a big disaster. The purpose of making jokes and humour is to take something which is perceived as scary and make it into a lighter, less scary thing. In other words, if you make a joke about cancer, you are trying to loosen its power over you by mocking it.

Therefore, my simple advice is to make sure that you use humour. Try not to put people down, but laugh at situations and try to make sure that you laugh with others. If one or the other of you is offended by the jokes, then what is happening is not working for you. However, if it is working for you, I would argue that it will help ease you through a very difficult situation.

In addition to humour there are various other ways of trying to discharge negative emotions and excess energy. Many people find writing helpful. I am sure the genesis of this book is in a psychological mechanism called intellectualisation. I wanted to write about some of the difficult things and to be practical for others as a way of dealing with my own emotions. In doing so, I found some comfort in taking what I learned from my dark experience and using it to provide some relief to others.

Most of you will not write a book, but writing is a tremendous tool. You can write about how you feel to get those feelings out. You can document your fears, hopes, goals, plans or anything else which may be useful.

I would also stress that it is not just writing that can assist – drawing pictures, writing poetry, and using various other types of art forms can all help to discharge negative emotion. Your goal is to survive this experience by letting go of as much of the emotion as possible.

Action Summary:-

- Humour is a useful device in discharging emotions. Make sure that you do not use it to ridicule people but use it to discharge fear and anxiety. Nobody else has to laugh as long as you do!

- Writing stories, journals and poems, as well as using art and creativity, are very useful tools for taking internal feelings and expressing them. Once they are out, it lowers their hold on you.

- How are you dealing with your emotions? If you are not talking to someone, use some mechanism to get your feelings out.

FUNERALS

A sad end point in this mortal life is ultimately death. Not only am I a psychologist, I have also worked as a lay minister and therefore conducted funerals. One of the things I have noticed is that some people are well-prepared, while others continue to avoid it to the end.

Among some of the best prepared funerals I have conducted, included that of a lady in her 80s who, about 5 years before she needed it, provided me with a complete programme of what she wanted in her funeral. This was someone who knew that dying was an inevitable part of life, and when she gave me the funeral programme she said she wanted to do it her way, and not the way somebody else wanted to do it.

Just like getting your affairs in order and travelling lighter, having a funeral plan has merit – it takes the weight off your family. If they know what your wishes and intentions are, it is one less matter for them to have to deal with later.

If you think it is too morbid or, as some people

consider it, making it too real, then of course follow the first rule of my book and do it your way. Therefore, do not worry about this chapter. However, for the families who have considered what should happen, their burdens are a lot lighter.

Action Summary:-

- Death is an inevitable part of being born into this world. When your time has come, it may not make any difference to you what happens at your funeral, but it will for your family.

- Preparation, while not always pleasant, is better than chaos for the family left behind. Have a plan. When you are well enough to stop and think about it, it is helpful to others.

CONCLUSION

Since your diagnosis, your perspective on the future has changed. You do not know how long you have. The practical reality is that everyone has a limited time on this earth – it is just that we kid ourselves that it will not end. Staring death in the face has brought home just how mortal you really are. That is a fearful and overwhelming experience, but it can also be a gift.

Why a gift? You now have the choice of making every minute count. Your minutes are precious and you can now choose to make the most of the time you have. The only thing which has changed is how much future you may have. Some people survive the treatment and go for years. For others it may be the cancer that brings home the finality of the situation.

It has been shown that trauma survivors who successfully address their psychological issues often end up in a better place emotionally than they were before the trauma occurred. It strengthens them and they find new meaning. The tricky part is the journey to get there when there is an ocean of issues

Conclusion

associated with cancer and the treatments which follow. My hope is that this book will help you to know that there is something to look for, and help prompt your journey in that direction.

I remember reading about a pioneer in the grieving process, Elizabeth Kubler-Ross. When asked how she coped with the work of helping people in the final stages of life, she spoke of stopping to watch the sunset each day. She said she had a special appreciation for the moment. That is the key to your journey, grab the moment (in Latin Carpe diem means "seize the day" – you do not need to seize it but please do not waste any moments).

I think that when times are tough there is a lot to be said for the natural world. Things like watching a sunset, walking on the beach, visiting the mountains, and seeing other places of nature and beauty all serve to ground us in the moment. Look at what is around you and focus on the beauty of the world.

My line of logic in this book is to make the most of the moments which are available. When I used to work in a juvenile remand centre, the young offenders would be upset about not knowing what was going to happen in court. There was to be a judgment, but they did not know what it would be. I used to say to them that you have no choice in the outcome, but you can choose to do your time easy or do it hard. You are in much the same position, in that you have no ability to change the final outcome, but the choice you have is whether to do your time easy or do it hard.

To do it easy, grab the moment, see the positive, and enjoy what you can. Every moment is precious and the gift you have is that your eyes have been opened to allow you that choice. Too many people take life for granted and put off what really matters. What are those things? To love and be loved, see the beauty, learn to be close to God, be at peace with yourself and others, and enjoy your limited time in this mortal toil. You have the choice to make the most of your time.

Now is the time to lighten your load and get rid of any excess baggage (material or psychological) you have collected in your life. It is a time to be you and make the most of your life now and in the future – whatever path it takes.

I wish you well in your journey and may your precious life be blessed.

Dr Phil Watts

Additional copies of

A psychological survival guide for breast cancer

are available from:
Ogilvie Publishing
PO Box 393
South Perth, 6951
Western Australia
Phone: 08 9450 1618
Fax: 08 9450 8618
Email: philpsyc@iinet.net.au
Website Order Form: www.drphil.com.au
Or
Online booksellers such as Amazon

www.ingramcontent.com/pod-product-compliance
Lightning Source LLC
Chambersburg PA
CBHW070625300426
44113CB00010B/1669